Funny Money

and

Honest Money

(A study into the viability of a Gold Standard in India)

Manish Thatte

manishjagdishthatte@gmail.com

Date: 3/10/2014

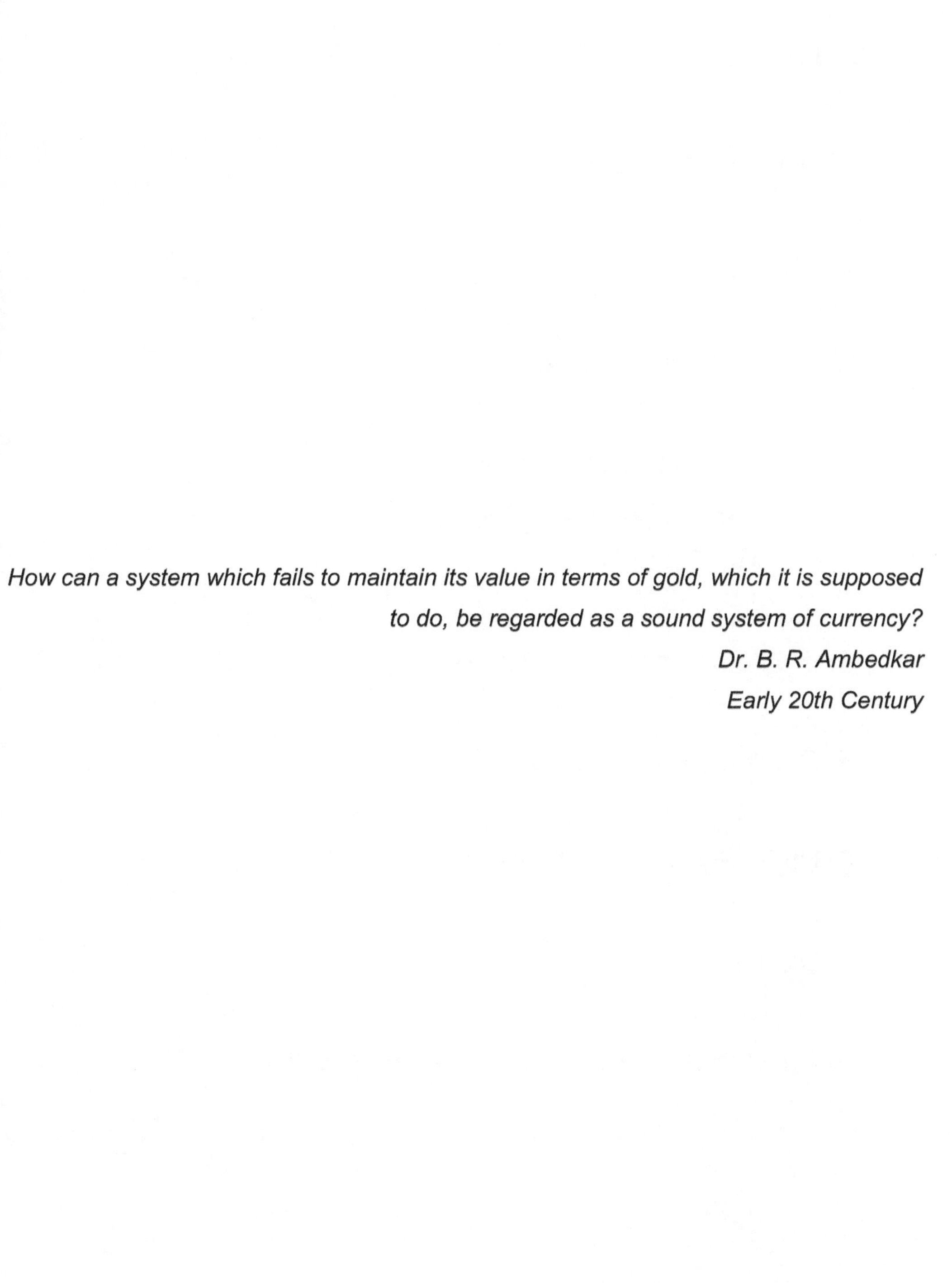

How can a system which fails to maintain its value in terms of gold, which it is supposed to do, be regarded as a sound system of currency?

Dr. B. R. Ambedkar

Early 20th Century

Index

0) What is money

I remember once, when I was a small boy, I went to purchase some clothes for myself with my parents. But my mother told me that first we have to go to the bank to take out some money for the purchase. I couldn't understand why was money needed from the bank when my parents always seemed to have money in their purses, neither did I understand from where did money in the bank come from.

So, where did my parents get money in their purses and where does the bank get the money, which it pays to us when we need it (of course, if and when we have a net savings balance in our account? There were no credit cards in those days.) And what will the cloth merchant do with our money?

Quite simply, my parents worked as businessman and employee, and from the profits of the business and salary which they got when the month was over, the money came.

This simple intercourse demonstrates that money is:

1) Remuneration for the goods and services provided to the community. (Think salary and profits)

2) Money is a store of work done previously, that is, it is a store of value. (Think bank accounts, fixed deposits etc.)

3) Money is medium of exchange i. e. It is the settlement or extinguishment of debt. (Think about the shopkeeper who sells his clothes in exchange for my money, and who in turn pays the cloth manufacturer and the tailor for their work and keeps some of the money as a profit / operating expense for himself).

So, money is three things, viz. medium of exchange, store of value and payment for useful work done. So, as a corollary, Anything else is not money.

What do we see today? Everybody and his grandma is purchasing a big expensive car on loan. Now a days, people seem to take a loan for almost anything, home loan, credit card loan, car loan, marriage loan, gold loan, foreign travel loan etc. India, a country which since times immemorial had been a financially healthy country of honest savers is being turned into a country of borrowers, decadents and consumerists.

The thought in my mind began taking root, that something was terribly wrong with today's monetary system. And hence the reason for this essay.

I researched the Internet to find out how we used to carry about our business in the ancient times and in the recent past in the world in general and in India in particular. And I came across the brilliant and well researched PhD. thesis of Dr. B. R. Ambedkar, as well as the works of such gifted scholars as John Maynard Keynes, Ludvig Von Mises, Murray N. Rothbard and Hugo Salinas Price. I also have the pleasure of being able to coordinate and obtain the valuable guidance of Dr. Vinayak Govilkar who had been my teacher during my MBA and continues to guide me to this day. I dedicate this very first of my work to the above mentioned scholars.

So, back to the point. What was right earlier and what is wrong with today's monetary system?

1) What is funny money

Fiat money (which I term as funny money) is currency which derives its value from government regulation or law. It differs from commodity money, which is based on a good, often a precious metal such as gold or silver, which has uses other than as a medium of exchange. The term derives from the Latin term 'fiat' ("let it be done", "it shall be").

History of Fiat Money: The first use of fiat money was recorded in China around 1000 AD. Since then, it has been used continuously by various countries, concurrently with commodity currencies.

Fiat money originated in 11th century China, and its use became widespread during the Yuan and Ming dynasties.

The Song Dynasty in China was the first to issue paper money, the jiaozi, around the 10th century AD. Although the notes were valued at a certain exchange rate for gold, silver, or silk, conversion was never allowed in practice. The notes were initially to be redeemed after three years' service, to be replaced by new notes for a 3% service charge, but, as more of them were printed without notes being retired, inflation became evident. The government made several attempts to support the paper by demanding taxes partly in currency and making other laws, but the damage had been done, and the notes fell out of favor.

The successive Yuan Dynasty was the first dynasty in China to use paper currency as the predominant circulating medium. The founder of the Yuan Dynasty, Kublai Khan, issued paper money known as Chao in his reign. The original notes during the Yuan Dynasty were restricted in area and duration as in the Song Dynasty.

During the 13th century, Marco Polo described the fiat money of the Yuan Dynasty in his book The Travels of Marco Polo.

All these pieces of paper are, issued with as much solemnity and authority as if they were of pure gold or silver... and indeed everybody takes them readily, for wheresoever a person may go throughout the Great Khan's dominions he shall find these pieces of paper current, and shall be able to transact all sales and purchases of goods by means of them just as well as if they were coins of pure gold.

—Marco Polo, The Travels of Marco Polo

Through out history various governments in Europe and Asia have been tempted to issue fiat currency of one kind or the other.

In the 20th century, after World War I, in theory, governments still promised to redeem notes in specie on demand. However, the costs of the war and the massive expansion afterward made governments suspend redemption in specie. Since there was no direct penalty for doing so, governments were not immediately responsible for the economic consequences of printing more money, which led to hyperinflation – for example the hyperinflation in the Weimar Republic.

From 1944 to 1971, the Bretton Woods agreement fixed the value of 35 United States dollars to one troy ounce of gold. Other currencies were pegged to the U.S. dollar at fixed rates. The U.S. promised to redeem dollars in gold to other central banks. Trade imbalances were corrected by gold reserve exchanges or by loans from the International Monetary Fund.

The Bretton Woods system collapsed in what became known as the Nixon Shock. This was a series of economic measures taken by the then United States President Richard Nixon in 1971, including unilaterally canceling the direct convertibility of the United States dollar to gold. Since then, a system of national fiat monies has been used globally, with freely floating exchange rates between the major currencies. What has exacerbated this problem is that various governments of the world have gotten into a habit, recently and currently, of issuing this paper money in the form of currency notes, coins and debt on an increasing scale (e.g. The QE programs).

So, what are the peculiarities of fiat money? Lets see some of them:

1) Nobody worked to provide useful goods and services and / or generate profits, which they paid to the government as taxes, and then the government issued those accumulated taxes as notes, coins or loans to deserving individuals. i.e. The Government just brought some money into existence by literally crediting the account of its central bank with some numbers or electronic digits.

2) Such fiat money was also not any store of value, which the past generations had worked hard and earned, and then passed on their legacy to the government to spend at a future date.

3) It may be tempting to call Such fiat money as a medium of exchange, in the sense that it is counted in Rupees, Dollars, Euros and Pounds, but remember, its not real money in the sense that there is no backing to it either in terms of past or present useful work done.

At best such money may be seen as a promise given by its receivers for the future valuable work which they are going to do.

It is akin to the shopkeeper giving me the clothes without me giving him anything in exchange, perhaps a promise to pay him at a future date, the price of the clothes. But once I get possession of the clothes, the shopkeeper has no means to ensure that me or my parents will pay the price. And by the way, I (the voter) have a lot of sutali firecrackers (votes) saved from the last Diwali, which I can use to cause nuisance to the shopkeeper if and when he insists on payment.

So, in essence, fiat money grows on trees (money plants anyone?) or it can be created out of nothing or in the extreme, it can even be dropped from helicopters (think helicopter Ben) so that the people will take it and spend it to get useful goods and services. Lets take a look at some of the various kinds of funny monies that are circulating around the world today.

Rupee: The rupee is the common name for the currencies of India, Pakistan, Sri Lanka, Nepal, Mauritius, Seychelles, Maldives, Indonesia (as the rupiah), and formerly those of Burma and Afghanistan and even the United Arab Emirates. Historically, the first currency called "rupiya" was introduced in the 16th century by Sher Shah Suri, founder of the Suri Empire of Northern India. The term is from rūpya, a Sanskrit term for silver coin, from Sanskrit rūpá, beautiful form. It is also alternately said that the name Rupee originates from the Sanskrit word Rupyakam (a unit of money measurement in Ancient Akhanda Bharat (Akhanda Bharat refers to todays India, Pakistan, Sri Lanka, Nepal, Bangladesh, Bhutan, Mauritius, Seychelles, Maldives, Indonesia , Thailand, Malaysia, Singapore, Burma and Afghanistan.) **The Sanskrit word for silver is Roupya!!!)**

The original rūpaya was a silver coin weighing 178 grains (11.534 grams or 1 tola). As Dr. Ambedkar has noted in his seminal work, the rupee minted at various mints across the country during the Mughal period was standardized, to a very high precision.

Name of the Rupee	Weight in pure Grains	Name of the Rupee	Weight in pure Grains
Akbari of Lahore	175.0	Delhi Sonat	175.0
Akbari of Agra	174.0	Delhi Alamgir	175.0
Jehangiri of Agra	174.6	Old Surat	174.0
Jehangiri of Allahabad	173.6	Murshedabad	175.9
Jehangiri of Kandhar	173.9	Persian Rupee (1745)	174.5
Shehajehani of Agra	175.0	Old Dacca	173.3
Shehajehani of Ahmedabad	174.2	Muhamadshai	170.0
Shehajehani of Delhi	174.2	Ahmadshai	172.8
Shehajehani of Delhi	175.0	Shaha Alam (1772)	175.8
Shehajehani of Lahore	174.0		

So, we see, that as recently as the Mughal era, for which we have hard data, there was a silver rupee weighing approx 11.5 grams and a gold mohur of similar weight for higher value transactions.

The Indian Government used to hold about 350 tons of gold in its vaults till Nov. 2009. But in November 2009, India purchased 200 tons of gold, due to dollar weakness taking its total official gold holdings to about 550 tons. And Indian citizens and temples hold about 20,000 to 25,000 tons of gold in private hands, and about approximately, 200,000 tons of silver in private hands, by some estimates.

Pound Sterling: The pound is a unit of currency in UK. The term originated in Great Britain as the value of a pound (2.2 kilograms in weight) of silver. The word pound is the English translation of the Latin word libra, which was the unit of account of the Roman Empire. The British pound derived from the Roman libra, which is why the pound (mass) is often initialized to 'lb'; along with the French livre, the Italian lira and the Portuguese Libra.

The UK officially holds about 200 tons of gold.

Euro: The euro (sign: €; code: EUR) is the currency used by the Institutions of the European Union and is the official currency of the eurozone, which consists of 18 of the 28 member states of the European Union: Austria, Belgium, Cyprus, Estonia, Finland, France, Germany, Greece, Ireland, Italy, Latvia, Luxembourg, Malta, the Netherlands, Portugal, Slovakia, Slovenia, and Spain. Lithuania is adopting the euro as its official currency in place of the lithuanian litas on 1 January 2015. The name euro was officially adopted on 16 December 1995. The euro was introduced to world financial markets as an accounting currency on 1 January 1999, replacing the former European Currency Unit (ECU).
The Euro was never based on any precious metal to derive its value from. It was floated freely against the worlds currencies, particularly the US Dollar.

But today, the EU as a conglomeration of nations continues to officially hold the largest stock of gold in its central banks, particularly Germany and Italy.

Ruble: Historically, a "ruble" was a piece of a certain weight chopped off a silver ingot (grivna), hence the name. Another version of the word's origin is that it comes from the Russian noun рубец, rubets, i.e., the seam that is left around the coin after casting: silver was added to the cast in two steps. Therefore, the word ruble means "a cast with a seam".

Russia officially holds about 1,000 tons of gold.

Right up-to WWII the pound, ruble and many other currencies were linked to gold and silver by weight.

Yuan (Renmimbi): The renminbi is the official currency of the People's Republic of China. The name literally means "people's currency".

The yuan is the basic unit of the renminbi, but is also used to refer to the Chinese currency generally, especially in international contexts. The distinction between the terms "renminbi" and "yuan" is similar to that between sterling and pound, which respectively refer to the British currency and its primary unit.

The yuan was the People's money espoused by Mao in the 1960s. It was never linked to gold and / or silver at anytime, except in antiquity.

China currently and officially holds about 1,000 tons of gold in its reserves.

Dollar: The word Dollar originates from the word Thaler. On 15 January 1520, the kingdom of Bohemia (it was then a state located in today's Czech Republic in Central Europe) began minting coins from silver mined locally in Joachimsthal. The coins were called "Joachimsthaler," which became shortened in common usage to thaler or taler. The German name Joachimsthal literally means Joachim's valley or Joachim's dale. This name found its way into other languages: Czech tolar, Hungarian taller, Danish and Norwegian (rigs) daler, Swedish (riks) daler, Icelandic dalur, Dutch (rijks) daalder or daler, Ethiopian talari, Italian tallero, Polish talar, Persian Dare, as well as – via Dutch – into American English as dollar.

The USA is officially the largest holder of gold in the world and continues to hold about 8000 tons of gold in its vaults.

History of the US Dollar: The history of the dollar is more interesting and enduring. Initially the dollar was a certain weight of gold and silver. The dollar was freely and fully convertible in gold and silver. That is, you could freely demand a certain weight of gold or silver in exchange for the dollars which you submitted to the American Federal Reserve.

In the 1930s, President Roosevelt made it illegal for Americans to own any personal gold, ostensibly, so as to put that gold to use to come out of the depression. At that time the dollar was exchangeable with gold at the rate of 20 USD for every ounce of gold. After the domestic confiscation of the gold, the US changed the rate of the dollar from 20 USD per ounce to 35 USD per ounce for international transactions. (Meaning a straight profit of 75% for the American Federal Reserve and the American Government).

After the WWII, the economies of Europe and Japan had been severely damaged and war-ravaged. USA was the only country which still had a modicum of sense as a normally functioning economy. At the Bretton Woods Conference, it was agreed by all the Major countries to base their individual currencies on the dollar, and the fully convertible dollar was to be based on gold at the rate of 35 dollars per ounce of gold. That rate remained steady till 15th August 1971, when President Nixon closed the gold window to the world. Now, the dollars earned by the other countries (by export to the US) could not be redeemed for gold. These countries were stuck with their dollar reserves.

Rise of the petrodollar: In the meanwhile during the Korean War, Vietnam War and the Cold war, America also realized, (following in the footsteps of Prof. Keynes) that the gold standard will never allow it to run up financial deficits. And financial deficits are necessary if you want to finance a war in a far off place.

Also, the real power behind smoothly running the wheels of the modern economic world was not gold but easy and cheap energy. So, America signed an agreement with Saudi Arabia (house of Saud) that whatever crude oil that Saudi Arabia will sell, it will be priced in the dollar !!! And in return, USA guaranteed the House of Saud, that they will not be destabilized from their ruling position. This single contract was to give rise to the hegemony of the Petro-Dollar for years to come in the future.

So, now which ever country depended on crude oil (that makes it most of the countries in the world) from the middle east, had to first have dollars to pay to the middle east countries. So, first they had to earn those dollars by exporting what ever goods and services they had to USA! Now all countries began a mad scramble to export their own commodities, goods and services to America. So, as a bonus to America, all the international trade of goods, commodities and services came to be priced in dollars.

This is the intrinsic power and value of the American Dollar which is continuing to this day!

But this phenomenon also had a sad side effect. It hollowed out the industries and services sector of the USA. What was once a very well developed and industrialized nation at the end of the WWII, has now become dependent on other countries, mainly The People's Republic of China, for almost all its product and services needs. The major production and export of the US is today USD and dollar denominated bonds.

WWI: So, we see that most major countries were on some sort of a gold and/or silver standard till world war I. What happened during the WWI?

How did the gold standard fail during WWI?

During periods of very high demand such as World War I, the countries involved, needed an unlimited supply of ammunitions and war equipment in order to win. A victory is unattainable if the gold needed to finance the seemingly limitless demand for war equipment is in short supply. This war scenario is equivalent to an expanding economy where people's desire for goods and services are boundless, but without a boundless supply of capital this cannot be attained and would always lead to a contraction. Countries involved in the war abandoned the gold standard, at least temporarily to accommodate the limitless demand that gold cannot keep up with.

But since World War I happened during the industrial revolution, noting that efficiency for producing goods was exponentially increased, prices of goods should continue to decline, then why was the gold standard unable to deliver the required demand? The answer may lie in the technological capacity to produce the required ammunition. The seemingly unlimited demand for war equipment reveals a quota or limit to the quantity of items that a single equipment can produce per a designated amount of time. Meaning, if 20 machines can make 10,000 bullets a day and bullets are consumed in the front lines at a rate of 50,000 per day, extra machines and man power are needed to accommodate that demand. This would mean that extra workers and equipment are needed to produce 50,000 bullets. If the daily cost to manufacture 10,000 bullets is $100,000, then producing 50,000 bullets requires the manufacturer to buy 80 more machines and hire more workers causing the daily production cost to increase to $500,000. It is now obvious that the marginal cost to produce extra bullets to meet the demand would require additional capital and thus more gold. This enormous demand coupled with the boundaries of technology would definitely stagnate production if extra capital is not obtained. Gold restricts this mega expansion and the gold standard was suspended for a fiat currency system during the WWI, by the main protagonist countries of WWI.

Currently, all the currencies mentioned above are what we can call fiat currencies, or funny money in the sense, that their monies do not possess any intrinsic value of their own. Their value is stamped by their government and is accepted and circulated by the general public, solely on the basis of trust in the underlying economy and the honesty of the issuing government.

2) What is honest money

Now that we have seen what is fiat money, it is very easy to postulate what honest money is. Namely, in addition to other qualities, it must possess 3 most essential qualities...

1) It must be a really long term store of value and must not be perishable

2) It must be able to reimburse honestly for valuable goods and services provided

3) It must be able to extinguish debt with finality

It so happens, that since the dawn of civilization, various monies have been in use such as cowries (shells), salt, cattle, bags of grain, gold and silver (gold mohurs and hons and silver rupyakam). Of these, since the gold and silver coins fulfill all the above conditions unobtrusively, and have been doing so since times immemorial, let's focus on them.

As of today, silver is a commodity and is also liable to get tarnished in polluted and humid climates. So let's not consider silver at the moment. Also, silver along with platinum and palladium have industrial uses such as making catalytic converters, critical for modern living. So, why waste physical silver, platinum and palladium as a currency or store of value?

Which leaves us with gold. Gold possesses all the above much needed characteristics. In addition to that, it has zero utility (except a very minor utility in electronics) aside from its use as jewelry. Gold is as if nature herself has handed over an ideal medium of exchange (currency) to humanity. Also, its unique density and rarity makes it very difficult to counterfeit. Also, it very primly satisfies the three conditions namely,

1) Gold does not tarnish, neither does it corrode, it is not perishable, so it is a really long term store of value.

2) It cannot be printed at will by any central bank. So, unless, you have gold over which you really have in your own right, you cannot pay somebody. So it is able to reimburse honestly for valuable goods and services

AND

3) It is not any promise to pay the bearer as assured sum of money promised by any bank or government. Thus, it is an excellent medium to extinguish all debt with finality.

Gold also has other excellent qualities such as almost unlimited divisibility, universal fungibility, luster, rarity, high weight to value ratio etc.
In addition to that, whatever fluctuations and new discoveries were to happen in the gold mining sector have almost all been past. And now, on an average the net annual addition to the world's gold stocks is 2% of the total. (Well, of course, if transmutation of heavy metals into gold becomes economically viable, then this hypothesis will collapse.)

Thus, it will even appeal to classical Keynesian economists, that the rate of inflation in a gold standard will be a steady, benevolent and gentle 2% per annum, all other things being equal.

Dr. B. R. Ambedkar, in his treatise, classifies the masses into three types, the savers, the employers and the employee. We can conclude, that a gold mohur will be an ideal medium to save money, purchase machinery and set up industries with and will also be suitable to pay the employees which they in turn can spend to satisfy their daily needs.

3) Types of honest money

Now that we have seen what honest money is and have discussed some of the effects, lets see how can we get back to the gold standard aka the honest money system?

a) Specie

In the *gold specie standard* the monetary unit is associated with the value of circulating gold coins or the monetary unit has the value of a certain circulating gold coin. Quite simply it means the government mint will mint standardized gold coins of requisite purity and weight, and they will be acceptable as legal tender in the open market and for government payments.

The reader will appreciate at the outset, that in such a system the gold coins in circulation will be liable for wear and tear in daily usage. Hence this is not suitable, at-least initially, according to some economists. This author is of the view, that Gresham's law will operate. If and when a freely convertible, free floating and legal tender gold mohur is introduced into the marketplace, alongside of paper currency notes, first of all it will be hoarded. Let it be hoarded by the people. It will give them that much more monetary stability. The money belongs to the people and so it should be in their own hands.

b) Gold Exchange Standard

The *gold exchange standard* usually does not involve the circulation of gold coins. The main feature of the gold exchange standard is that the government guarantees a fixed exchange rate to the currency of another country that uses a gold standard (specie or bullion), regardless of what type of notes or coins are used as a means of exchange. This creates a de-facto gold standard, where the value of the means of exchange has a fixed external value in terms of gold that is independent of the inherent value of the means of exchange itself.

So, if tomorrow US or UK or China or Russia starts relying on a gold standard and we peg our Rupee at a fixed rate to the USD, Pound, Yuan or Ruble respectively, that will be as good as a gold standard, as long as the reference country does not debauch its currency by any means. Before the Nixon Shock of 1971, most countries of the world were on such a gold exchange standard. The chance of that happening in the near future is very remote at best.

c) Gold Bullion Standard

The *gold bullion standard* is a system in which gold coins do not circulate, but the authorities agree to sell gold bullion on demand at a fixed price in exchange for currency.

This according to the author, is the ideal system at the moment for our country. But it will be a test of patience of our central bank and the ruling government to see to it that there is no inflation and the gold notes are truly honored.

d) Bi-metal Standard or even multiple commodity standard

In this case, gold and or silver and or copper and or aluminum or even a basket of energy and commodities may be used as a basis to issue currency. But such a case is too complicated to consider at the moment, hence we will treat it at a later stage.

4) Problems with funny money

When a country espouses the fiat standard, it adds to the number of "moneys" in existence. In addition to the commodity moneys, gold and silver, there now flourish independent moneys directed by each government imposing its fiat rule. And just as gold and silver will have an exchange rate on the free market, so the market will establish exchange rates for all the various moneys. In a world of fiat moneys, each currency, if permitted, will fluctuate freely in relation to all the others. We have seen that for any two moneys, the exchange rate is set in accordance with the proportionate purchasing-power parities, and that these in turn are determined by the respective supplies and demands for the various currencies. When a currency changes its character from gold-receipt to fiat paper, confidence in its stability and quality is shaken, and demand for it declines. Furthermore, now that it is cut off from gold, it's far greater quantity relative its former gold backing now becomes evident. With a supply greater than gold and a lower demand, its purchasing-power, and hence its exchange rate, quickly depreciate in relation to gold. And since government is inherently inflationary, it will keep depreciating as time goes on. Such depreciation is highly embarrassing to the government – and hurts citizens who try to import goods.

Lets see some of the gross problems which a fiat money in an economic system causes:

a) Wild fluctuations in the markets (Hyperinflation, stagflation, depression)

We have been witnessing various abnormal phenomenon in the financial markets since 1971, such as hyperinflation (Zimbabwe), the stock market bubbles of 2000, 2014, the Asian financial crisis, Crisis in Argentina, Financial crisis in USA in 2007-2008 etc. These are all due the unhealthy tendency of the world central banks to simply print money and loan money to the governments and corporates and individuals. Such money does not have any backing in terms of its not being any stored value. Its just printed or digitized into existence. So, its easy money, free money.

Whenever, such money is created, it tends to lower the value of honest money, because both are counted in the same unit of measure e. g. the Rupee. In such a scenario, what happens is, capital is not efficiently allocated to the most profitable ventures, but such capital goes to finance bubbles in various markets such as real estate (e. g. Freddie mac and Fannie may), stock markets (2000 and 2014 stock indices) etc. Greed feeds on itself and prudent financial decisions and investments are put on the back-burner.

b) The loot of the masses (investors, employers, employees and dependents)

When the central banks and the governments retain the power to issue their own money, they can be partial to their favored class of people and crony capitalists. They can benefit only those people and organizations which they favor. As a corollary, those people who are not of a favored status, see the value and purchasing power of their savings and investments being continually inflated away, when inflation runs rampant in a fiat monetary regime. Arbitrarily increasing the quantity of currency in an economy distorts the distribution of money and, therefore, redistributes purchasing power, effectively stealing wealth from the majority, e. g., savers and wage workers, to serve the interests of a privileged minority. Redistribution of wealth, as opposed to production of wealth, causes a net loss of wealth to society. Government deficit spending, although it may be motivated by good intentions, changes the quantity of currency and results in currency debasement. Thus, government deficit spending operates as a dishonest, hidden tax on savers and wage workers. In his well known 1966 essay, Gold and Economic Freedom, former Federal Reserve Chairman Alan Greenspan, wrote:

"Deficit spending is simply a scheme for the confiscation of wealth. Gold stands in the way of this insidious process. It stands as a protector of property rights. If one grasps this, one has no difficulty in understanding the statists' antagonism toward the gold standard."

c) Wars

N. M. Rothschild is said to have once uttered "I care not what puppet is placed upon the throne of England to rule the Empire on which the sun never sets. The man who controls the British money supply controls the British Empire, and I control the British money supply".

In today's scenario, the central banks and the governments of the world, control this money supply.

See, gold in the hands of the masses is real wealth and power in their hands. Gold is the ultimate democratization of wealth. And history is a witness, no democratic country has ever been an aggressor. Aggression is always committed under the sway of ambitious dictators and despots.

Let's take the case of India. Throughout history, India has never invaded any country what so ever. This is because, most of the real wealth i. e. gold and silver has always been under the control of its citizens. Real money is needed to finance wars. And real money goes into hiding at the first cloud of a war. Its not about being unpatriotic, its about being prudent.

As against that, consider Germany under Hitler, or more recently USA. The Federal Government of USA controls the money supply of its people; nay, of the whole world. And it is incessantly engaged in some kind of conflict with some or the other nation.

So, funny money tends to cause wars. As against that, real wealth or gold / silver in the hands of a country's citizens is the ultimate democratization of wealth.

d) Unreasonable asset bubbles:

What are asset bubbles? Wikipedia defines "An economic bubble (sometimes referred to as an asset bubble, speculative bubble, a market bubble, a price bubble, a financial bubble, a speculative mania or a balloon) is "trade in high volumes at prices that are considerably at variance with intrinsic values". It could also be described as a situation in which asset prices appear to be based on implausible or inconsistent views about the future.

Because it is often difficult to observe intrinsic values in real-life markets, bubbles are often conclusively identified only in retrospect, when a sudden drop in prices appears. Such a drop is known as a crash or a bubble burst. Both the boom and the burst phases of the bubble are examples of a positive feedback mechanism, in contrast to the negative feedback mechanism that determines the equilibrium price under normal market circumstances. Prices in an economic bubble can fluctuate erratically, and become impossible to predict from supply and demand alone.

In the 1970s, excess monetary expansion after the U. S. A. came off the gold standard (August 1971) created massive commodities bubbles. These bubbles only ended when the U. S. Central Bank (Federal Reserve) finally reined in the excess money, raising federal funds interest rates to over 14%. The commodities bubble popped and prices of oil and gold, for instance, came down to their proper levels. Similarly, low interest rate policies by the U. S. Federal Reserve in the 2001–2004 are believed to have exacerbated housing and commodities bubbles. The housing bubble popped as sub-prime mortgages began to default at much higher rates than expected, which also coincided with the rising of the fed funds rate.

Today, as of this writing, we are seeing a similar asset bubble in the real estate and stock markets, due to the pumping of liquidity by the various central banks of the countries of the world.

It is an undisputed fact that bubbles are caused due to excessive monetary expansion. A gold standard keeps a check on monetary expansion, as against that, a fiat money system is conducive to cause bubbles in various asset classes from time to time, depending on the mood of the speculators.

e) Price Instability: Fiat currencies, because they require relatively insignificant physical economic inputs, have no direct relationship to the survival requirements of human life. Since it is decided by central planners, the quantity of currency in a fiat currency scheme is always and inevitably incorrect. This causes price instability and artificially stimulates or depresses economic activity as a function of how much currency is produced and of how it is controlled and distributed. As a practical matter, price stability can never be achieved in a fiat currency scheme.

Long-term price stability has been described as the great virtue of the gold standard. The gold standard limits the power of governments to inflate prices through excessive issuance of paper currency. Under the gold standard, high levels of inflation are rare, and hyperinflation is nearly impossible as the money supply can only grow at the rate that the gold supply increases. Economy-wide price increases caused by ever-increasing amounts of currency chasing a constant supply of goods are rare, as gold supply for monetary use is limited by the available gold that can be minted into coin. High levels of inflation under a gold standard are usually seen only when warfare destroys a large part of the economy, reducing the production of goods, or when a major new source of gold becomes available. In the U. S. one of those periods of warfare was the Civil War, which destroyed the economy of the South, while the California Gold Rush made large amounts of gold available for minting.

f) The gold standard provides **fixed international exchange rates** between those countries that have adopted it, and thus reduces uncertainty in international trade. Historically, imbalances between price levels in different countries would be partly or wholly offset by an automatic balance-of-payment adjustment mechanism called the "price specie flow mechanism." Gold used to pay for imports reduces the money supply of importing nations, causing deflation and a reduction in the general price level for goods and services, making them more competitive, while the importation of gold by net exporters serves to increase the money supply, causes inflation and an increase in the general price level, making them less competitive.

g) The gold standard acts as a **check on government deficit spending** as it limits the amount of debt that can be issued. It also prevents governments from inflating away the real value of their already existing debt through currency devaluation. A central bank cannot be an unlimited buyer of last resort of government debt. A central bank could not create unlimited quantities of money at will, as there is a limited supply of gold.

h) A gold standard cannot be used for, what economists call, **financial repression**. Newly printed money can be used to purchase goods and services, and to discharge debts, at no cost to the printer. This acts as a mechanism to transfer the wealth of society to those that can print money, from everyone else. Financial repression is most successful in liquidating debts when accompanied by a steady dose of inflation, and it can be considered a form of taxation. In 1966 Alan Greenspan wrote "Deficit spending is simply a scheme for the confiscation of wealth. Gold stands in the way of this insidious process. It stands as a protector of property rights. If one grasps this, one has no difficulty in understanding the statists' antagonism toward the gold standard." Financial repression negatively affects economic growth and market sentiment.

i) The gold standard **benefits savers** by preventing their savings from being devalued or destroyed through inflation, and by rewarding them with higher real (inflation adjusted) interest rates. In the US and United Kingdom, from 1945 to 1980 negative real interest rates have cost lenders an estimated 3-4% of GDP per year on average.

k) The gold standard tends to **limit credit booms and the resulting boom bust cycle** because of the inelastic supply of money. There is no central bank to print ever increasing amounts of money which act as fuel for the boom, and overextended banks fail sooner as there is no central bank to bail them out, causing credit to contract and ending any booms that do occur.

5) Problems with honest money

A gold standard is not without its own problems. But compared to the problems caused by fiat money, such problems with the gold standard are not insurmountable. Lets consider what are the problems with a gold standard.

a) Fraud and Theft

Gold specie is subject to fraud. In the sense that the issuing authority or even unscrupulous individuals can adulterate the gold coin, as we have seen in the long history of the world since the Roman Empire.

This can be easily surmounted in 2 ways:

1) Technology: Modern technology has made it possible to have cheap and portable X-ray machines. I envisage a dharam-kata combined with an X-ray machine, to test the purity of the gold coins in circulation. Such a dharam kata maybe as common as we used to have STD booths.

2) Gold Bullion Standard obviates the need to have pure gold coins in circulation. As long as the RBI is freely and openly ready to exchange its currency notes for pure gold coins, there is no need to circulate gold coins. The gold can be stored across various locations across the length and breath of India e. g. The gold can be stored in the treasury branches of the State Bank of India in each district. That will also democratize the holding of wealth of the nation.

Alternately, each treasury branch can have a government certified mint, to mint gold coins freely or with a certain nominal seignorage, from the gold which the public brings to it.

Specie is also subject to theft, but then so are funny money notes.

b) Hoarding

Gresham's law states that bad money drives out good money out of circulation. It will be logical, if the RBI embarks on a policy of degrading its gold coins, or if the price of gold in the international markets skyrockets, then people will tend to hoard the gold coins they already have.

So, what I suggest is that the value of the gold coins not be stamped on them in Rupees, because the price is subject to change over time. The coins or bars can just have the weight and true purity stamped on them.

We need to understand here, that gold is the most unproductive asset. It just sits there and does nothing. Its not like real estate, or shares or bonds. It does not earn interest, dividend, rent, nothing. On the contrary, it is expensive and risky to maintain stocks of gold.

If the free market forces compel the people to hoard their coins without interest for indefinite periods, with the accompanying risk of theft, then fine. Other wise they may opt to lend them or deposit them with the banks, as a fixed deposit or for safekeeping. In a truly free market, the market forces will operate and people will be ready to bring their gold into circulations, as long as their gold earns the true market interest, when owned and gets the value in terms of useful goods and services, which it deserves from time to time when exchanged.

I am sure, hoarding will not be a problem, if the gold is valued properly from time to time. The key to this will be again I emphasize, not assigning any face value to the gold coin. Let the coin or bar find its own worth in the open market.

c) Banking and Fractional reserve banking:

Fractional-reserve banking is the practice where a bank holds reserves (to satisfy demands for withdrawals) that are less than the amount of its customers' deposits. Reserves are held at the bank as currency, or as deposits in the bank's accounts at the central bank. Because bank deposits are usually considered money in their own right, fractional-reserve banking permits the money supply to grow beyond the amount of the underlying reserves of base money originally created by the central bank.

Let us suppose a businessman comes to the bank and wants to borrow Rs. 1,00,000 to cover the cost of some additional inventory he wants to purchase. The bank may approve the loan, and the businessman will tell the bank to credit the Rs. 1,00,000 to his deposit account.

Bank Assets

debit Loans Rs. 1,00,000

Bank Liabilities

credit Deposits Rs. 1,00,000

The businessman now has an additional Rs. 1,00,000 demand deposit. No one else's demand deposits have been reduced. This is clearly an increase in the money supply, and it is apparent that the bank created the Rs. 1,00,000.

These derivative deposits are important both quantitatively and theoretically – it is in terms of derivative deposits that banks can be thought of as creators of money. If all deposits arose from primary deposits, banks could not be said to create money.

As stated earlier, **fractional reserve banking** will have to go. This may seem a bit stringent at the moment, but when the dust has settled, it will be seen to be most prudent. In the sense, that it will guarantee the financial solvency of the banks.
We may even speculate, that initially, a severe deflation will be caused in the real estate and stock markets, if the existing gold is not valued properly at market value.
When gold is monetized, either of the 2 things will have to happen, either gold will need to be valued to its true market value (here the government does not need to do anything, only let the free market forces play out, so that existing gold supplies find their true value) OR face deflation. By the way, deflation of asset prices is not a bad thing. What it will do is, it will negate the inflation that has become so rampant recently. But when the dust has settled, so to speak, we will be on the threshold and ready to usher in a golden stable age of banking, trade and commerce in India.
And of course, banking can be carried out in all its wonderful glory under a gold standard. What stops that from happening. Only thing is the banks will have an absolute liability to stay solvent, liquid and viable at all times. No Funny Money business, no window dressing, no favoring the undeserving.

d) Balance of Trade (import and export)

Today the position is that oil is priced in dollars. And oil is the lifeblood of trade and commerce. So, each and every nation is obliged to export goods and services to USA to earn dollars. (And as a corollary, USA exports its dollar papers and dollar electronic digits to the whole world. But we do not concern ourselves with that at the moment.) Under a gold standard, we can sign supply contracts with the oil producers. And I am sure, the oil producing countries will be more than happy to import the best of the best of Indian Spices, cloth, silk, gold jewelry, perfumes, fruits, dry fruits, vegetables, grains and various other goods, commodities and valuable services, which we can offer, in exchange for their oil. We can even use the price of the oil and our commodities and services in dollars as a reference. Same mechanism can be used to import other commodities and services from other countries and export our commodities and services to them. What ever the minuscule difference in the trade balance, can be settled in terms of gold and silver bullion, instead of paper fiat currencies, quarterly, half yearly or annually. I am sure, this will provide a great impetus to international trade between India and other countries. As a bonus, it will be an added incentive for Indians to start producing ever better goods and services, so that we don't have to let go of our precious gold reserves. In fact that's how Ancient India grew so rich in the first place.

e) Quantity of money needed

As stated earlier, my hypothesis is that gold and silver are currently grossly undervalued in relation to the underlying global economy. If and when we espouse the gold standard, 2 things can happen.

1) Deflation: No need to fear the word so much. By deflation, I mean, the bubbles which have been blown up due to the funny fiat money in various markets, such as commodities, real estate, stocks, bonds will need to be deflated to their true value in terms of gold and silver. Inflation is inflammation, it is not true growth. In the long run, a certain amount of deflation will prove to be very healthy for the economy.

2) Revaluation of gold and silver: Gold and silver, as money, will need to show an increase in their ability to purchase other commodities, real estate and stocks. In simple terms, if we don't want large scale deflation in the asset markets, then gold and silver will need to be revalued to higher levels in terms of their purchasing power.

In my opinion, if the free market forces are left to operate on their own, without government policy intervention, then an equilibrium will be soon reached as to the prices of the commodities, stocks, bonds, real estate and gold / silver markets. In simple terms, a combination of both, deflation and revaluation of purchasing power of gold and silver will occur.

f) What about Welfare Economics and stimulus?
Welfare Economics:
Wikipedia defines Welfare economics as that branch of economics that uses micro-economic techniques to evaluate well-being of the people(welfare) at the aggregate (economy-wide) level. A typical methodology begins with the derivation (or assumption) of a social welfare function, which can then be used to rank economically feasible allocations of resources in terms of the social welfare they entail. Such functions typically include measures of economic efficiency and equity, though more recent attempts to quantify social welfare have included a broader range of measures including economic freedom (as in the capability approach) and The Happiness Index of nations.

In the open society, there are some sections of the populace which require support, in the sense, that they are not able to provide for themselves e. g. the destitute, the old and the infirm.

Various governments across the world profess to help them and thus justify their printing of fiat money. But this is a falsity on their part. Printing fiat money makes the poor even more poorer, without their realizing that the government is taxing them without their knowing that they are being taxed. In a fiat money regime, only those who have easy access to the newly printed fiat money, e. g. The whole vertical value chain of the car spare parts supplier, the car manufacturer, the car dealer and finally the car purchaser benefits but the general population does not benefit in any way. And if the government attempts to benefit everybody at the same time then only the price levels increase as we saw in 2011 when the prices of grains and vegetables skyrocketed in India, when the Government increased the minimum support price of grains and vegetables. And this especially hits hard the poor daily wage earners, the retirees, the infirm and the destitute.

Government is free to do welfare economics to favored sections of society using the honest money taxes which they collect from honest tax payers. And in return, honest money tax payers will become more careful regarding whom to choose to govern themselves. As a bonus, suicides by the poor marginal land holding farmer will be severely curtailed, the influence of private money lenders will be severely curtailed, as the farmer farm laborer will now be able to earn and save honest money. His saved honest money in terms of gold and silver coins will come to the rescue as and when needed and that too with all its full purchasing power glory.

Stimulus: In economics, stimulus refers to attempts to use monetary or fiscal policy (or stabilization policy in general) to stimulate the economy. Stimulus can also refer to monetary policies like lowering interest rates and quantitative easing.

Often the underlying assumption is that due to a recession the production and hence also the employment are far below their sustainable potential due to lack of demand. It is hoped that this will be corrected by the increasing demand and that any adverse side effects from stimulus will be mild.

Fiscal stimulus refers to increasing government consumption or transfers or lowering taxes. Effectively this means increasing the rate of growth of public debt except that, particularly Keynesians, often assume that the stimulus will cause sufficient economic growth to fill that gap partially or completely by the money multiplier effect.

Monetary stimulus refers to lowering interest rates, quantitative easing, or other ways of increasing the amount of money or credit.

I am sure, that in an honest money regime, economic stimulus by deficit financing won't be needed. Of course, government can undertake many developmental projects (including construction of dams, canals, townships, metros, freeways, roads etc.) for the general uplift of society in general, but in the absence of deficit financing and fractional reserve banking that will have to be done through means of honest money. I am sure, that the private gold and silver holders will rise to the occasion. Our financial markets are now sufficiently mature. And I am also sure, that the foreign countries will see that the mere word of The Government of India is as good as gold. Many many countries will be very eager and will come forward to invest their precious finances and know-how in to a Golden Re-surging India. Especially when offered a chance in invest in the economy of a rich, powerful and peaceful country which can export so many valuable commodities, goods and services to them.

g) The total amount of gold that has ever been mined has been estimated at around 1,80,000 metric tons and arguments have been made that this amount is **too small to serve as a monetary base.**

h) The **unequal distribution of gold as a natural resource** makes the gold standard much more advantageous in terms of cost and international economic empowerment for those countries that produce gold. In 2010 the largest producers of gold, in order, are China, followed by Australia, the US, South Africa and Russia. The country with the largest reserves is Australia.

i) Although the gold standard has brought long-run price stability, it has also historically been associated with **high short-run price volatility**. It has been argued by, among others, Anna Schwartz that this kind of instability in short-term price levels can lead to financial instability as lenders and borrowers become uncertain about the value of debt.

k) **Deflation punishes debtors**. Real debt burdens therefore rise, causing borrowers to cut spending to service their debts or to default. Lenders become wealthier, but may choose to save some of their additional wealth rather than spending it all. The overall amount of expenditure is therefore likely to fall.

l) Mainstream economists believe that economic recessions can be largely mitigated by increasing money supply during economic downturns. Following a gold standard would mean that the amount of money would be determined by the supply of gold, and hence **monetary policy could no longer be used to stabilize the economy in times of economic recession**. Such reason is often employed to partially blame the gold standard for the Great Depression, citing that the Federal Reserve couldn't expand credit enough to offset the deflationary forces at work in the market.

m) **Monetary policy would essentially be determined by the rate of gold production**. Fluctuations in the amount of gold that is mined could cause inflation if there is an increase or deflation if there is a decrease. Some hold the view that this contributed to the severity and length of the Great Depression as the gold standard forced the central banks to keep monetary policy too tight, creating deflation.

n) James Hamilton contended that the **gold standard may be susceptible to speculative attacks when a government's financial position appears weak**, although others contend that this very threat discourages governments engaging in risky and populist public policy. For example, some believe that the United States was forced to contract the money supply and raise interest rates in September 1931 to defend the dollar after speculators forced Great Britain off the gold standard.

o) **If a country wanted to devalue its currency, a gold standard would generally produce sharper changes than the smooth declines seen in fiat currencies**, depending on the method of devaluation.

p) It is **difficult to manipulate a gold standard** to tailor to an economy's demand for money, providing practical constraints against the measures that central banks might otherwise use to respond to economic crises. The demand for money always equals the supply of money. Creation of new money reduces interest rates and thereby increases demand for new lower cost debt, raising the demand for money.

6) Discussion:

This author is of the opinion that the sooner we implement the gold standard the better, as otherwise, if there is any local or global black swan event, we will be left with a completely unstable and unusable financial system, and nobody knows if and when we will be able to get out of that quagmire???

How might we be able to implement the gold standard in today's times of daily, some or the other, technological innovation and invention?

Keynesians quickly dismiss gold as a barbarous relic. But cant we find some way out? Some via-media to implement something which has been successful for the past thousands of years of human history? In place of the dicey fiat money proposition and a virtual dream with which we have been deluding ourselves with?

In fact, the gold standard is better suited to function in today's economy than it was when it last operated, thanks to advances in technology that can more closely relate paper money with gold. Furthermore, after a 20th century of ill-conceived re-implementations and false starts, there is the benefit of experience at our disposal to craft a gold-based monetary system that is sturdy against external pressures and accountable to the people.

At the core of a gold standard is the principle of gold itself as functional money. If gold is to form the basis of a monetary system, it cannot be restricted in usage as money or demonetized as property. Otherwise, the promise of a paper currency's redemption in gold will be hollow. In short, gold needs to have the same legal tender status as the Rupee. How might that be possible? 1) **The taxation of money essentially demonetizes it, altering its fundamental character from being a medium of exchange to being merely another form of property – in the words of Utah legislator Larry Hilton.** First and foremost, the government should stop treating gold as an asset or commodity and start treating it as actual money. So, all taxes on holdings of gold and transactions in gold should be stopped. e. g. Wealth taxes, VAT, LBT, Capital gains taxes (long term and short term).

2) There is a company named GOLDMONEY, in the British Channel Islands. They have found a way to monetize gold. What the company does is, it accepts deposits of gold

from its customers and issues them a **debit card** up to the value of their gold in fiat money. The customers can replenish their balance by depositing additional gold or instructing the company to purchase gold on their behalf, spend their balance at commercial establishments, check their gold balance etc. i. e. carry out all normal banking transactions which we can carry out with a normal fiat money account.

So, if and when gold is monetized, such debit cards will come into vogue. Banks may even able to issue gold based credit cards, to their customers. So, basically, the gold standard is just as simple that one fine morning we start treating gold as actual money. And that will be that. No great immediate social or political upheavals are feared by this author, except the higher revaluation of gold and silver in the markets and a bit of deflation in speculative assets such as real estate, stocks and bonds.

3) War and Peace: As seen through out history, a stable monetary system has always broken down during times of national emergencies, upheavals, war, earthquakes, excessive rainfall, riots, droughts etc. in short "asmani" and "sultani" causes. That is true even for balance of trade during fiat currency regime. It will be no different than that if and when we are on a gold standard. In all such cases better policing will be and always has been a solution.

7) Who others are on a gold or silver standard?

There is always space at the top. Currently, no sovereign country is on a gold or silver standard. Right up-to the Bretton Woods Agreement, almost all countries were on a gold or silver standard. After The Bretton Woods Agreement, only the USA was on a gold standard, and all the other country's currencies were pegged to the USD, right up-to 15th August 1971. On 15th August 1971, President Nixon closed the gold window by executive order, thus ending the free convertibility of the USD with gold. After that, gold was free to float in terms of the currency of each country. This paved the way for Keynesian policies to run rampant in the world. Keynes was a brilliant economist, and his policies were perfect for a World War Ravaged Europe to come out of the quagmire of the severe damage caused by the Great War. But today, in times of peace, his policies have lost their relevance. On the other hand, the world has created an artificial black-hole of fiat currency and derivatives. Its high time that we came to realize that nature never intended humanity to print their way out of debt. That's not the way how nature works, not in physics, neither in chemistry and never in biology. There are no free lunches.

Utah, Malaysia, Mexico and Switzerland:
Utah: Utah is a state in The USA. In 2011, Utah passed a law and legalized the use of gold and silver coins as legal tender in addition to the American Federal Notes.
Malaysia: Malaysia is a Muslim country and it wants to implement Sharia Law in its monetary system. Malaysia is in the process of incorporating and implementing a silver dirham into its currency system.
Mexico: Mexico has introduced the silver 'libertad' as currency in parallel with the circulation of its peso.
Switzerland: Switzerland is holding a referendum of its citizens to compel its central bank to hold 20% of its reserves in gold on 30th November 2014. In effect, if the referendum passes through, the Swiss Franc will become a 20 % gold backed currency.

INDIA: India can now lead the way by launching a full fledged gold standard. We can convert some of our huge stockpile of 300 billion USD reserves into gold. These reserves are paying a minuscule interest at the moment. And god forbid, if the USD collapses as it is bound to collapse anytime, under its own weight of 17 trillion dollars of US national debt, what will happen to our balance of payments?

At the current market price of USD 1200 for 30 grams of gold, even if we purchase a few hundred tons of gold, we will still have sufficient USD to pay our oil bills.

6) Conclusion

Let's not forget, that the people of India are some of the wisest people in the world. Over the past many centuries, they have squirreled away an estimated 25,000 tons of gold, (more but not less) and an immeasurable quantity of silver. I am sure, that all that gold and silver will come in circulation once gold and silver is legislated as the legal tender and India becomes a gold standard country.

Traditionally, Ancient India has been a rich nation. It used to be called a 'Sone ki Chidiya'. i. e. A golden Bird. There is a reason for that!!!

Many an ancient economists (especially Romans) have lamented that all that India sends us is her spices and silk which are perishable commodities but what India accepts in payment is only Gold and Silver. That gold and silver is still out there, among the Indians. Only thing is it needs security and stability to come out into circulation. This is a golden opportunity for India to reclaim its developed and prosperous nation status among the countries of the world.

The author suggests that to begin with The Government should stop its fiat money policies immediately. Let the rupee appreciate against the dollar and other currencies. If other nations want to do quantitative easing of their own, let them do that. Though, the Author recommends and predicts that most other nations will see the infallible logic in the above arguments, and fears that they will adopt a gold standard long before these arguments reach the higher echelons of India's finance ministry.

Exports will suffer initially. But in the place of valuable exports in exchange for funny looking paper notes and electronic digits, we will have a golden chance to improve our own commodities, products and services and get something valuable in return for them.

And what we have in our favor is the young and vibrant population of India. The demographic dividend so to speak.

At least the farmer suicides will stop. And with its appreciating currency and high demographic dividend, India will become a magnet for foreign investment. But mind well, we are preparing to usher in a gold standard. So, we will only accept investments in gold and / or oil and natural gas. ☺

We should peg the value of the rupee to be backed by 100% gold and silver (say at the nominal market rate of Rs. 30,000 per 10 grams and Rs. 40,000 per kg of silver) as of today.

Initially, the Government may introduce a very high value (say Rs. Ten lakhs or Rs. One Crore) note which will be fully convertible and backed by gold and a One lakh Rs. note in equivalent quantity of silver) with the RBI. Roughly it works out to a gold brick of 333.33 gms. and 3.3333 Kg. and a silver brick of 2.5 Kg. A high value note is essential initially, so as to facilitate better checks on tax evasion, money laundering. And if people want to hoard such a brick, they are welcome. Remember, the brick will never be said to have gone out of circulation, only it will be squirreled away for any contingency.

Such a note and the corresponding bullion coin / bar can even be marked with an RFID tag. Such a note may also be invested in a bank so as to earn interest and on maturity again become fully convertible in gold. In addition, such a note may also be made compulsory to pay taxes / government dues by the corporates / individuals. Or alternately, a small discount maybe offered on payment of taxes by means of gold and silver notes. This is sure to bring in much needed supplies of gold and silver stock in to the public treasury.

Later-on smaller denominations of paper notes and coins fully backed by gold, silver and copper may be brought into circulation. This topic will be discussed at length at a later date.

Bibliography

1) The Problem of the Rupee - Dr. B. R. Ambedkar

2) What has Government done to our Money - Murray N. Rothbard

3) Man, Economy and State (A treatise on Economic principles) - Murray N. Rothbard

4) Wikipedia

5) Hugo Salinas Price - www.plata.com.mx/mplata